*S*tepping to the brink of Grand Canyon begins a lifelong challenge for the geologist, biologist, ecologist, archaeologist, historian, and theologian. Ordinary people become extraordinary students in this "Library of the Gods," for the Grand Canyon is universal in its many lessons. None of us is ever quite the same for having experienced its gifts, precious treasures to carry forever in our memories.

*M*ather Point on the South Rim is
the first view many visitors have of
Grand Canyon. Cliffs plunge a
vertical mile below and a ribbon of
water courses its way west on the
canyon floor, while a pervading
sense of dimension staggers
the imagination.

Grand Canyon National Park, *located in northern Arizona, established in 1919, preserves the finest continuous geologic record on earth.*

Front cover: Zoroaster and Brahma Temples, photo by Jeff Gnass. Inside front cover: Stormy afternoon from Point Imperial, photo by Kaz Hagiwara. Page 1: Canyon view from Mather Point, photo by Gary Ladd. Pages 2/3: Morning at Mather Point, photo by Gary Ladd. Pages 4/5: Passing storm at Hopi Point, photo by David Muench.

Edited by Cheri C. Madison
Book design by K. C. DenDooven

Fifth Printing, 1993
in pictures GRAND CANYON The Continuing Story
© 1990 KC PUBLICATIONS, INC.

LC 90-60038. ISBN 0-88714-046-7.

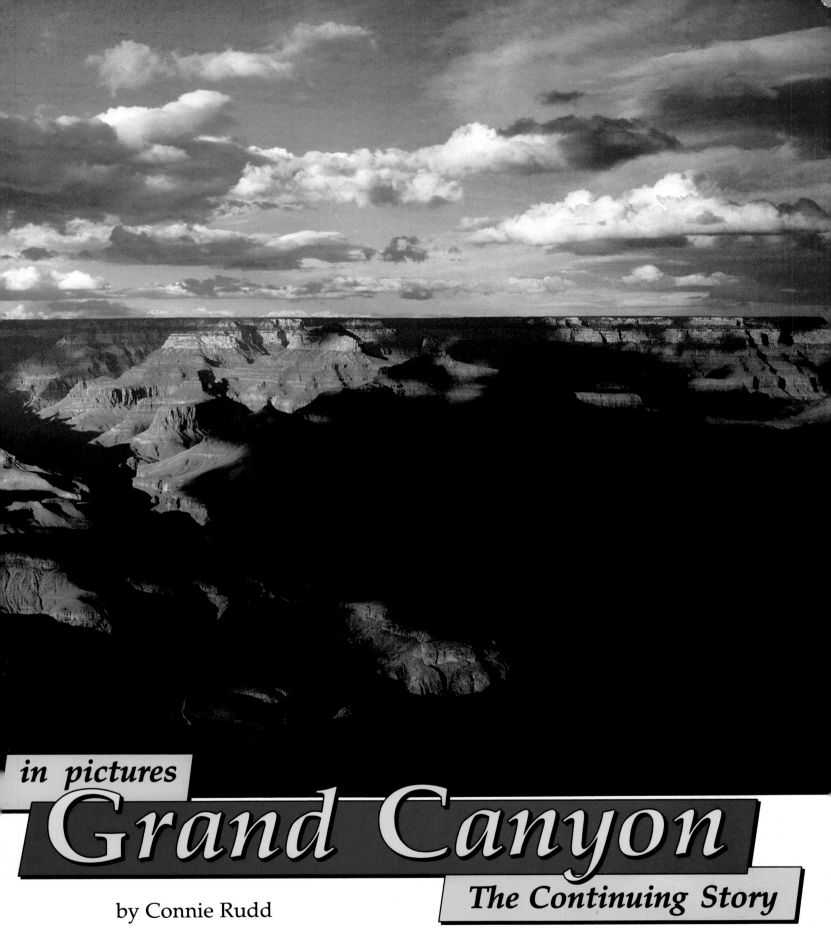

in pictures
Grand Canyon
The Continuing Story

by Connie Rudd

Connie Rudd, a career employee of the National Park Service, served as Park Ranger-Interpreter at Grand Canyon between 1980-1989. She earned a B.A. in English at Ohio University and added graduate studies in physical geography at the University of Illinois. An author of children's publications, Connie also wrote "Grand Canyon-North Rim: The Story Behind the Scenery."

National park areas are special landscapes set aside by acts of Congress to protect and preserve features of national significance that are generally categorized as scenic, scientific, historical, and recreational. As Americans, we are joint caretakers of these unique places, and we gladly share them with visitors from around the world.

On a clean, crisp day in bright sunlight, the edges of Grand Canyon are clearly evident, tricking us into believing that this landscape is measurable, definable. Its numbers are easy to read: 277 miles long, averaging 10 miles wide in the heart of the canyon, a mile deep, with rocks as old as 2 billion years, carved by relentlessly running water during the last 5 million years. But sheer numbers tell us little of the significance of the Grand Canyon. Science, philosophy, and art come together here, challenging each of us to define for ourselves the value of the region.

The South Kaibab Trail etches its way through a fresh snow as it descends the foreground ridge.

Water: The Creator

The Colorado River slices through a vertical mile of rock, chiseling slopes and free-standing temples and buttes. These are "the leaves of a great stony book," described by Major John Wesley Powell on one of the earliest explorations of the region in 1869. One glance told Powell that this was the single greatest page in earth history, and it was open for reading. Scholars may disagree about some aspects of the complex regional geology, but most agree about the role played by water: it certainly was responsible for the formation of the rock layers in the upper two-thirds of the canyon walls. They are comprised of alternating layers of sandstone, limestone, and shale—all sedimentary rocks deposited between 600 million and 250 million years ago. Deposi-

tional environments ranged from warm, shallow inland seas to coastal shorelines and damp swamplands, with the noted exception of the Coconino Sandstone, deposited under dry desert conditions. Grain by grain of sand, molecule by molecule of lime and mud, cemented together by the pressure of overlying layers and chemicals within water, solid rock was created from sediments left by ancient sources of water in the region. After these water-born rocks were layered on the heat-born rock of the inner gorge, and after the dinosaurs dominated the earth, the region was lifted thousands of feet above sea level, priming it for a profound period of erosion which would carve the Grand Canyon.

JOSEF MUENCH

◁ **Waterfalls, tucked in** remote side canyons, often with difficult access, transform a hot, dry journey into paradise. Deer Creek Falls tumbles 100 feet over the 550-million-year-old Tapeats Sandstone on the north wall of the canyon. These falls can be reached by raft from the river or by a three-day round trip hike from the North Rim through Surprise Valley.

Grand Canyon is ▷ reshaped with every passing storm. While the depth of the canyon was carved by the Colorado River, the width is the result of mechanical and chemical weathering, a process which includes freeze/thaw cycles, plant root wedging, gravity, and chemical changes due to rainwater and soil combinations. In a century the canyon may grow one inch deeper, but ten inches wider.

The Ever-changing Canyon

ED COOPER

△ **Capping both rims, the Kaibab Limestone gently sweeps to form a large** amphitheater between Cape Royal and Wotan's Throne on the North Rim. The scalloping effect of the canyon rims is created by rain- and melt-water spilling over the edges, etching headward, ever widening it. Called amphitheaters, these deep side canyons are most pronounced on the North Rim where accelerated erosion takes place due to increased precipitation at its higher elevations.

Angel's Window, on the North Rim's Cape Royal Road, represents the ▷ early stages of chemical and mechanical weathering which may ultimately create a stunning landform called a spire. Now connected to the rim by the limestone "bridge," the rock material to the left will eventually be isolated as the window below enlarges with each freeze/thaw cycle and as the rock chemically breaks down with each dose of rainwater. Six thousand feet below this window of time lies the Colorado River.

Geologic Time:
The Fourth Dimension

ED COOPER

DICK DIETRICH

◁ **Sculpted of 250-million-year-old Kaibab**
*Limestone, Duck on the Rock perches on the edge of
the East Rim Drive between Desert View and Grand
Canyon Village. Time has cracked off the "beak."*

Actual distance in the Grand Canyon has fooled many observers not familiar with its △
dimensions. Estimating size becomes a herculean task, especially after standing deep within the
canyon walls, surrounded by earth rising in every imaginable direction. Whether viewed from the
rims or experienced from within, a sense of the elusive fourth dimension is ever present: the
passage of geologic time. Here, in the eastern end near Desert View, with younger cliffs rising on
the northeast horizon, the painted desert unfolds to the east, representing a modern erosional
surface mantled with desert scrub: the ancient covered with the here and now.

Water: The Destroyer

With the regional uplift of the Colorado Plateau beginning some 65 million years ago, drainage systems began to establish themselves across the highlands. Water from snow melt and rain began coursing its way to the Pacific Ocean via a number of routes, stripping off thousands of feet of sedimentary rocks deposited on top of present-day rim rock. However, as recently as 6 million years ago, Grand Canyon had not yet been carved, and the Colorado River system as we know it had not yet evolved. With the opening of an arm of the Gulf of California about 5.3 million years ago, the course of the lower Colorado was established, reaching western Arizona and draining the present-day Grand Canyon region. River water, equipped with the erosive tools of mud, silt, pebbles, cobbles, and boulders, sliced through the rock layers, carving the Grand Canyon to approximately its present depth about 1.2 million years ago. A steep gradient still exists within the river channel, suggesting the canyon could become another 1,200 to 2,000 feet deeper if canyon carving should continue uninterrupted in the geologic future.

TOM TILL

△ *The sandstone which forms the walls in Deer Creek Gorge was deposited under coastal shoreline conditions 550 million years ago. Deer Creek has etched into this layer, defining the slightly softer from the more resistant bands within the Tapeats Sandstone.*

JEFF GNASS

◁ *Near Desert View, the confluence of the Colorado River with the Little Colorado River provides a spectacular contrast when the sediment load of each is different. With no suspended mud, the main river channel appears green.*

GARY LADD

The Colorado ▷
River encountered its toughest task in the latter stages of canyon carving ...working its way through the most resistant layers of metamorphic rock. Looking downstream from Plateau Point toward Horn Creek, the somber schists of the Vishnu Group form the steep walls of the inner gorge.

Ancient Life Clues

◁ **Clues to ancient environments are** *locked in each layer of rock, frozen in time to be discovered millions of years later. These tubeworm burrows in the Tapeats Sandstone are evidence of simple life on a coastal shore some 600 million years ago.*

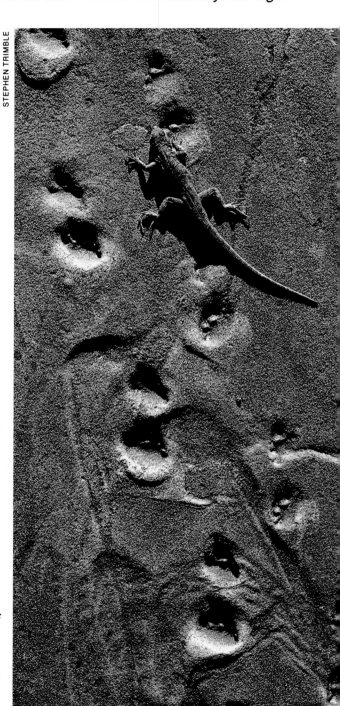

STEPHEN TRIMBLE

PETER KRESAN

Each layer from top to bottom is younger than ▷ *the one below it. Fossil evidence recreates a story of increasingly complex life forms as we move up the stratigraphic column. Here, tracks left by a heavy-bodied reptile some 270 million years ago are found in the Coconino Sandstone, the third layer from the top.*

As well as carving a stunning canyon, erosion in its many forms has revealed ▷ *layers of ancient life. Cliffs of harder limestones and sandstones and slopes of softer shales reveal fossils in each layer. Its relative position from top to bottom helps determine the age of each rock unit.*

△ **Forming the uppermost cliff in** the canyon, the Kaibab Limestone harbors an abundance of fossils, including brachiopods, corals, snails, sponges, clams, and sharks' teeth. This Meekella brachiopod is an example of easily-observed fossils on the surface of both the North and South rims.

△ **Fossil evidence is quite varied, from this** mineral-replaced brachiopod to impressions left in wet sand or mud of a fern, raindrop, mudcrack, or footprint, or even to the tissue-thin trace of a trilobite in the Bright Angel Shale.

River Red, River Green

Battling ▷ mighty Hermit Rapid, rafters bail out gallons of muddy Colorado River water. Following spring melt or a sudden rain-storm the Colorado turns its historic red-brown.

TOM TILL

◁ **Rafters** rest at Redwall Cavern along a peaceful Colorado River. The waters are impounded upstream behind Glen Canyon Dam, and most sediment is trapped in Lake Powell. Clear, cold water is released, fostering the growth of algae on the channel bottom which appear to color the water green.

LARRY ULRICH

▲ **Badger Creek flows intermittently, creating a rapid as it dumps debris into the main** channel after a rain. Without sufficient force during spring flooding, the Colorado River does not purge its rapids as often as before the building of Glen Canyon Dam. Canyon carving would continue if the river moved swiftly, carrying its load of mud, silt, sand, rocks, and boulders, rather than being choked with infrequently-moved material.

Toroweap: Remote Beauty

Vulcan's Throne ▷ at Toroweap thrusts its vegetated peak high, now a quiet remnant of the last period of volcanic activity. About one million years ago, molten lava in this vicinity cascaded over the canyon rim into the river.

◁ ***Plunging 3,000*** feet straight down to the river below, the canyon is perhaps at its most sheer in the western end. Accessible only by rough dirt roads, Toroweap Overlook includes a few modest picnic tables and a primitive campsite. The wind whistles past the canyon's edge most of the time, accentuating the remote splendor of this little-visited portion of the park.

Lava Falls, ▷ directly below Toroweap, is the most difficult to negotiate on the river, as it drops 37 feet within the rapid. River runners pause to plan strategy for a safe run.

ED COOPER

20

RAY ATKESON

Silver trunks and golden yellow aspen leaves, against deep green spruce and fir, create a forest medley at the edge of open meadows on the North Rim. At elevations above 8,000 feet, this rim supports a lush, diverse forest.

JEFF GNASS

◁ **Serving as "nurse"** trees, a clump of aspen shield a young blue spruce, providing necessary shade and soil. Eventually the spruce will overtake the aspen, producing a dense, shade-tolerant forest, suited to withstand the rigors of a North Rim winter.

North Rim:
The Canyon Beckons—
The Forest Holds You

GAIL BANDINI

GAIL BANDINI

△ **Ponderosa pine march right up to** the edge of the North Rim, stopping abruptly. Even a short hike along the Widforss Trail imparts unique lessons in forest ecology and canyon geology, blended nowhere better than here. Take bird books and flower books, as well as a fossil book.

△ **Drainage on the North Kaibab Plateau is not** well defined. Much of the water finds its way to internal sinks in the limestone where it may stand as it does during the wet season at Greenland Lake. Eventually it disappears, often reappearing as seeps and springs emerging from the canyon wall below.

Overleaf: From Point ▷
Sublime on the North Rim, a magic moment at sunset is electrified as a late evening storm rumbles away to the lower South Rim. Photo by Dick Dietrich.

23

JOHN RUNNING

△ **Several commercial river outfitters offer trips** of varying length on the Colorado, from 1-day flatwater excursions or week-long adventures to the ultimate 21-day, oar-powered expedition the entire 277-mile length of Grand Canyon. Expert river guides provide safe travel through the more than 100 rapids.

Running of the Grand

Leading the first successful expedition the length of the Colorado River in 1869, Major John Wesley Powell literally put Grand Canyon on the map. His report to Washington, D.C. included incredibly accurate maps, detailed if not "creative" illustrations, and a serious, scholarly explanation of the geology of the region. Today, more than 15,000 courageous people each year don life vests, equip themselves with several days' provisions, and step into rubber rafts or wooden dories to challenge the same Colorado River. These students of adventure still make discoveries: mostly about themselves, the fragile nature of wilderness, and their relationship to it. Protecting the grandness of this river environment is one of the most important jobs entrusted to the National Park Service.

◁ **Badger** Rapid is the first encountered below Lees Ferry. The ferry site serves as starting point for all river boats and is the zero point for measuring miles downstream. Badger Rapid is at river mile 8.

JOSEF MUENCH

C. ALLAN MORGAN

JOHN RUNNING

△ **Solitude is sought and found on the** Colorado River. Clocks have little use here, and most river travelers tuck their watches away for the trip's duration.

STEPHEN TRIMBLE

△ **Literally created overnight by a 1966 flash flood in** the Crystal Creek tributary, Crystal Rapid has become a technically difficult rapid to negotiate.

△ **Looking** downstream from the Nankoweap area, mile 52, beach development and erosion are in evidence. Beaches are cleansed and redeposited only during infrequent high water stages.

Constructed in ▷ 1928, the Kaibab Suspension Bridge spans the river just above Phantom Ranch at river mile 87.

CONNIE RUDD

Songs of Nature on the River

◁ **Emerging from** the Redwall Formation just above the river is Vasey's Paradise Falls, fed by underground springs originating on the North Rim. Major Powell named it for the botanist George Vasey who accompanied him in previous explorations.

Camp is made ▷ at Muav Gorge on ledges near river level. Thoughtful river management requires all travelers to leave no trace of their passing, taking everything with them, including the ashes from the campfire burned in a fire pan.

TOM TILL

DAVID EDWARDS

DAVID EDWARDS

◁ △ **Wilderness soothes the spirit, releasing** us from daily tensions.

TOM TILL

29

Life in the Canyon

"Everything is connected to everything else"— a basic principle of ecology, with complex implications. Grand Canyon is a superb laboratory for learning the relationships of all living things, including the positive and negative effects humans have on planet earth. The first detailed biological study of Grand Canyon was completed by Dr. C. Hart Merriam in the 1890s. Based on observations, he pieced together his concept of "Life Zones." Over time his notions have become more accurately called "biotic communities," as elevational and latitudinal changes encourage differences in plant and animal associations. Abundant life is found at every elevation within the canyon, from the cool, moist North Rim at 8,000 feet, to the hot, dry depths of Grand Wash Cliffs at 1,200 feet. Each plant and animal has adapted to its home environment and, without undue disturbance by human activity, lives well. But none lives unaffected by other life forms, because everything is connected to everything else.

GARY LADD

◁ **Springing** up from virtually no soil at all is brittlebush, a member of the sunflower family. A dominant shrub on and below the Tonto Plateau, it blooms with showy yellow flowers in late April. Native Americans chewed a gum produced in its stem, and it also serves as a food source for bighorn sheep.

△ **Bighorn sheep require large territories of rugged** cliffs and ledges for safety and survival. Their numbers were once seriously threatened by the introduction of domestic burros which became wild and overgrazed bighorn habitat. In 1981 the last of the burros were removed.

△ **Falcons and other birds of** prey are found in wild and remote areas of Grand Canyon.

◁ **Inextricably connected to the** ponderosa pine forest of the North Rim, the rare Kaibab squirrel makes a living harvesting pine nuts and inner bark from the trees. Found only on the North Rim, the Kaibab squirrel has a close cousin, the Abert, which occupies a similar ecological niche on the South Rim.

CONNIE RUDD

CONNIE RUDD

***F**ound in the inner canyon are two* △ ▷
*similar-looking desert plants. The narrow-
leafed yucca on the left, a member of the lily
family, produces creamy white blooms each
year. Native Americans used its fibrous leaves
for rope and sandals, its root as soap or
laxative. The Utah agave on the right, a
member of the amaryllis family, blooms only
once in its 20-30 year lifetime, then dies. Its
roots were roasted for food or fermented
into an alcoholic beverage.*

Plant Life

◁ **Carmine** thistles are found on both rims and are an important food source for hummingbirds.

In stunning ▷ counterpoint to its surroundings, the beavertail cactus (a subspecies of the prickly pear) produces magenta blooms in April and May in the inner gorge. Packrats rely on its seeds, while its roots inexorably wedge canyon rock into the river below.

DAVID MUENCH

PAUL VUCETICH

△ **Coral fungus hastens** the decomposition of downed timber on the North Rim.

GARY LADD

Maidenhair fern clings to cracks ▷ opened by water seeps at Shower-Bath Spring in Kanab Canyon. The fern is most lush in spring.

△ **This birdwatcher should look on his cap for** the nearest feathered creature. Quietly blending into the environment has its advantages.

MARY EDWARDS WERTSCH

△ **A mountain chickadee** forages seeds on a dried mullen plant.

C. ALLAN MORGAN

LYNN CHAMBERLAIN

△ **The male western** tanager is one of the most brightly colored birds seen on or just below both rims.

C. ALLAN MORGAN

This immature male black- ▷ chinned hummingbird feeds on flower nectar and occasional insects. By beating their wings more than 60 times per second, hummingbirds hover over flowers to dip long tongues for sweet treats.

◁ **Mule deer browse on a large variety of** plants as their source of food. Deer populations on the North Rim took a dramatic dive in the 1930s following the attempted eradication of major predators by government scouts. Without predators, herd size first increased and then plummeted when food sources could no longer support the animals. Wildlife management now calls for natural cycles of checks and balances to regulate animal populations.

ERWIN & PEGGY BAUER

▽ **As a defense against** predators, the chuckwalla lizard inflates its leathery body with air while in a rock crevice, wedging tightly so it cannot be easily extracted.

C. ALLAN MORGAN—DRK PHOTO

C. ALLAN MORGAN

△ **Spotted skunks are sometimes seen in the** inner canyon by backpackers. Less aggressive than their striped cousins on the rims, the spotted can have the same odorous effect on the campsite.

The Havasupai

Though geographically a part of Grand Canyon, Havasu Canyon, a major tributary west of Grand Canyon Village, is on the Havasupai Indian Reservation. Descended from the rim-dwelling Hualapai tribe, the modern Havasupai live in a canyon paradise. Their name means "people of the blue-green water," aptly describing their dependence on the mineral-rich creek of turquoise water which flows through the reservation. The Havasupai were primarily an agricultural society 300 years ago, raising crops and livestock. Today, agriculture still plays a role, but subsistence is augmented by healthy tourist traffic.

DICK DIETRICH

Havasu Falls plunges 100 feet to ▷ travertine terraces below. Suspended in water, the mineral travertine later deposits as ledges.

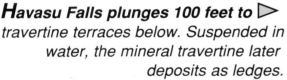

DIANNE DIETRICH LEIS

◁ **Four major** waterfalls are within a few trail miles of each other as Havasu Creek descends to the Colorado River. The creek provides habitat for waterfowl, hummingbirds, beaver, bighorn sheep, and ringtails.

A rugged hiking ▷ trail parallels the creek on its descent, passing Mooney Falls. Plant and animal life abound in the narrow riparian zone associated with this year-round water source.

GARY LADD

A *typical January snow reaches about* △ *2,500 feet below the rim to the top of the Redwall Formation.*

Winter in Grand Canyon

Snow settles on the North Rim by the end of October, closing it for the rest of the season. The South Rim is blanketed with occasional snow between December and April, but remains open. The warmer inner canyon rarely receives snow, however, making the contrast between the rims and river spectacular. Winter precipitation is a vital source of water for both plants and animals at all elevations within the canyon. A handful of cross-country skiers visit the North Rim, while many ranger-guided activities continue on the South Rim.

DIANNE DIETRICH LEIS

◁ **Spring** *is frosted by late snowfall* at Mather Point.

The *quiet of winter settles on* ▷ *Lookout Studio in Grand Canyon Village.*

Discover Grand Canyon on Your Own

For many visitors, standing on the rim of Grand Canyon is not enough. There is something compelling about the complexities of the inner canyon that attracts hundreds of thousands to venture further. Some are satisfied with a day hike below the rim, others return every year for extended treks in the remote backcountry. Hiking in this canyon will test each person both physically and mentally. These are not leisurely strolls, but difficult, cardiovascular workouts. Proper preparation is a lifesaving must, and permits are required for all overnight stays below the rim. The single most important item carried by any hiker is water, followed by food and portable shade in the form of hats and long sleeves. Please check with a park ranger before attempting any of Grand Canyon's rigorous trails.

GARY LADD

△ **The South Kaibab Trail descends** directly to the Colorado River over a course of seven miles. It is steep, lacks shade and water, is considered difficult, and is recommended only for downhill treks.

Here backpackers revel in the solitude of ▷ the narrows of Jumpup Canyon, a tributary of Kanab Creek, accessible from the North Rim. Flash floods in the usually dry tributary creeks are always a possibility during the summer monsoon season.

GARY LADD

MARK E. GIBSON

Bright Angel △
Trail is the oldest and
most popular inner
canyon route from the
South Rim. Rest
houses, seasonal
water, and some
shade make it
appealing.

◁ **G**uided mule rides
offer an alternative to
hiking the dusty canyon
trails. Offered by
concessioners on both
rims, mules can be hired
for day or overnight
excursions. It is wise to
make reservations early.

ED COOPER

KENT & DONNA DANNEN

△ **Photographing the many moods of Grand** Canyon could take a lifetime. Sunrise and sunset are favorite times to rim-watch, whether in the company of a dog, alone, or with others. Low light enhances photos shot at this time of day. Pets are permitted on the Rim Trail only and must be leashed.

◁ **A short hike down historic Bright Angel Trail** reveals a tunnel chiseled through the limestone. Established first as a toll road at the turn of the century by the enterprising Ralph Cameron to protect mining claims, it is now part of the National Trails System.

◁ **Early** South Rim rail passengers stayed in the elegant El Tovar Hotel opened by the Fred Harvey Company in 1905. Rail service, begun in 1901, ceased in 1968 but was revived in 1989, with historic passenger trains making frequent runs from Williams, Arizona.

DICK DIETRICH

MIKEL CONRAD

*R*anger-guided walks are offered throughout the △ year. Park rangers share the story of Grand Canyon with visitors from around the world. A complete list of programs is available in "The Guide" newspaper and is posted at the visitor centers.

◁ *F*riendly rangers on horseback always attract a crowd. Protecting the park for future generations is part of the National Park Service mission.

CONNIE RUDD

CONNIE RUDD

△ *T*he Junior Ranger Program for young visitors is available year-round. Ask at any information desk for details.

KENT & DONNA DANNEN

◁ *S*ometimes a walk alone on the Rim Trail teaches the best lessons of self-discovery.

43

JOSEF MUENCH

△ **More than 4 million visitors worldwide come each year to experience Grand Canyon. As** *decisions are made to manage this "Wonder of the World," perhaps it is best to keep in mind the words spoken by President Theodore Roosevelt on his first visit in 1903: "Leave it as it is....The ages have been at work on it, and man can only mar it....Keep it for your children, your children's children, and for all who come after you, as the one great sight which every American...should see."*

Grand Canyon Natural History Association

Chartered by Congress in 1935 as a non-profit organization to aid interpretive and research programs, the Grand Canyon Natural History Association offers financial support to many park efforts, including the Junior Ranger Program and the publishing of an extensive list of interpretive materials. Memberships are available at all bookstore outlets in the park visitor centers.

SUGGESTED READING

EULER, ROBERT C., and TRINKLE A. JONES. *A Sketch of Grand Canyon Prehistory.* Grand Canyon, Arizona: Grand Canyon Natural History Association, 1979.

HUGHES, J. DONALD. *In the House of Stone and Light.* Grand Canyon, Arizona: Grand Canyon Natural History Association, 1978.

PRICE, L. GREER. *Grand Canyon: The Story Behind the Scenery.* Las Vegas, Nevada: KC Publications, Inc., 1991.

RUDD, CONNIE. *Grand Canyon-North Rim: The Story Behind the Scenery.* Las Vegas, Nevada: KC Publications, Inc., 1989.

WHITNEY, STEPHEN. *A Field Guide to the Grand Canyon.* New York: Quill Press, 1982.

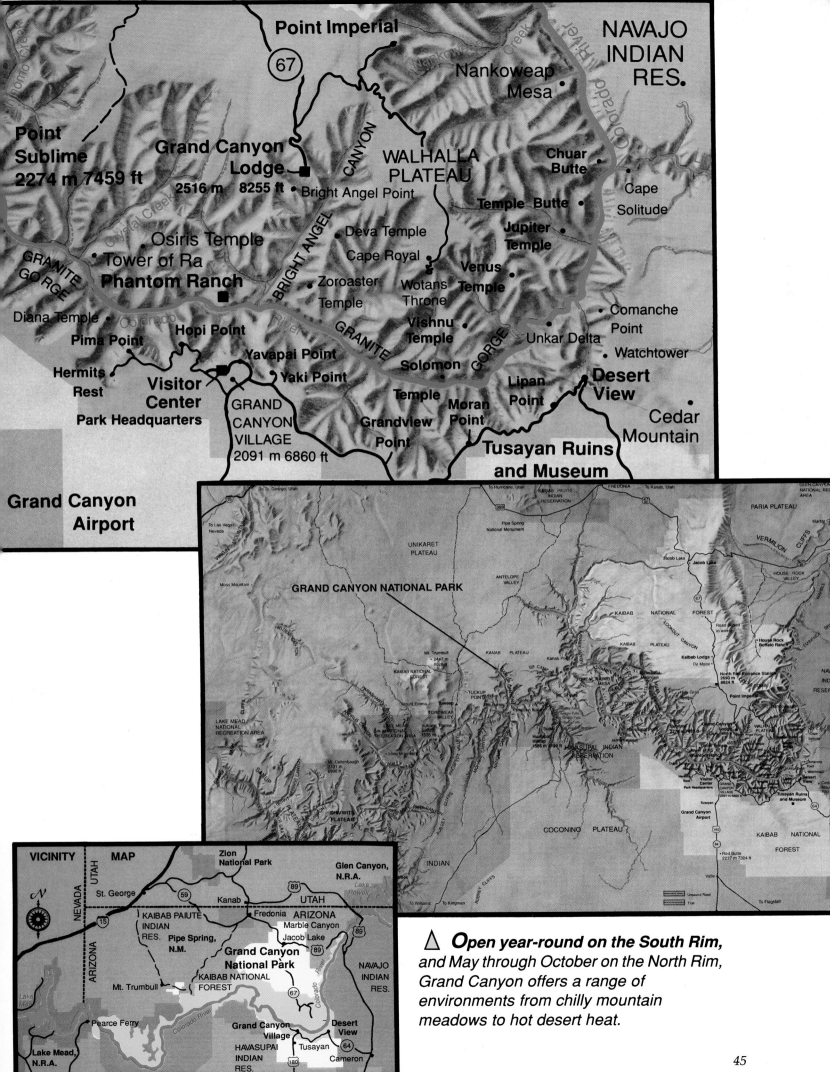

NAVAJO INDIAN RES.

Point Imperial

67

Point Sublime 2274 m 7459 ft

Grand Canyon Lodge 2516 m 8255 ft
• Bright Angel Point

Nankoweap Mesa

WALHALLA PLATEAU

Chuar Butte •

• Cape Solitude

BRIGHT ANGEL CANYON

Temple Butte •

• Deva Temple

Jupiter Temple •

GRANITE GORGE

• Osiris Temple
• Tower of Ra
Phantom Ranch

Cape Royal

Venus Temple •

Diana Temple •

• Zoroaster Temple

Wotans Throne

Vishnu Temple •

• Comanche Point

Hopi Point

• Unkar Delta

• Watchtower

Pima Point

Yavapai Point

Solomon

GRANITE GORGE

Hermits Rest

• Yaki Point

Temple

Lipan Point

Desert View

Visitor Center

GRAND CANYON VILLAGE 2091 m 6860 ft

Grandview Point

Moran Point

Park Headquarters

Tusayan Ruins and Museum

Cedar Mountain

Grand Canyon Airport

VICINITY MAP

Zion National Park

Glen Canyon, N.R.A.

NEVADA | UTAH

St. George

59

Kanab

UTAH

Lake Powell

NEVADA

15

KAIBAB PAIUTE INDIAN RES.

Pipe Spring, N.M.

Fredonia

Marble Canyon

Jacob Lake

ARIZONA

89

89

ARIZONA

Grand Canyon National Park

NAVAJO INDIAN RES.

Mt. Trumbull

KAIBAB NATIONAL FOREST

67

Colorado River

Pearce Ferry

Grand Canyon Village

Desert View

Lake Mead, N.R.A.

93

Tusayan

Cameron

HAVASUPAI INDIAN RES.

180

64

To Williams and Flagstaff

89

△ **Open year-round on the South Rim,** *and May through October on the North Rim, Grand Canyon offers a range of environments from chilly mountain meadows to hot desert heat.*

45

The Paiute Indians, who lived on the North Rim, have a single word which describes all of Grand Canyon: it is "kaibab." Kaibab means "mountain lying down" or "mountain inside out," and carefully considered, that tells us all we need to know. Our relationship to this land—past, present, and future—is a continuing story of connections. Every one of us is a steward of this land, connected to its health and its intrinsic riches, and is responsible for passing it on to the next generation. What you take in your mind and spirit from your visit to Grand Canyon will last a lifetime. Its diverse lessons of nature have global connections, and if we listen to the passage of time whispered among these canyon walls, larger truths may be known, in this mountain lying down.

WILLARD CLAY

A piñon pine stands as sentinel on the South Rim near Mohave Point.

DIANNE DIETRICH LEIS

△ **Sunrise from the South Rim implies continuity and order in the natural world.**
It is there for the taking—all the lessons the earth has to teach. Let Grand Canyon be the grand instructor. You be the grand learner.

NEW: in pictures—The Continuing Story: Arches & Canyonlands, Bryce Canyon, Death Valley, Everglades, Glacier, Glen Canyon-Lake Powell, Grand Canyon, Hawai'i Volcanoes, Mount Rainier, Mount St. Helens, Olympic, Petrified Forest, Sequoia & Kings Canyon, Yellowstone, Yosemite, Zion.
This *in pictures* series is available in translation packages.

Books in The Story Behind the Scenery series: Acadia, Alcatraz Island, Arches, Biscayne, Blue Ridge Parkway, Bryce Canyon, Canyon de Chelly, Canyonlands, Cape Cod, Capitol Reef, Channel Islands, Civil War Parks, Colonial, Crater Lake, Death Valley, Denali, Devils Tower, Dinosaur, Everglades, Fort Clatsop, Gettysburg, Glacier, Glen Canyon-Lake Powell, Grand Canyon, Grand Canyon-North Rim, Grand Teton, Great Basin, Great Smoky Mountains, Haleakala, Hawaii Volcanoes, Independence, Lake Mead-Hoover Dam, Lassen Volcanic, Lincoln Parks, Mammoth Cave, Mesa Verde, Monument Valley, Mount Rainier, Mount Rushmore, Mount St. Helens, National Park Service, National Seashores, North Cascades, Olympic, Petrified Forest, Redwood, Rocky Mountain, Scotty's Castle, Sequoia & Kings Canyon, Shenandoah, Statue of Liberty, Theodore Roosevelt, Virgin Islands, Yellowstone, Yosemite, Zion.

Published by KC Publications • Box 94558 • Las Vegas, NV 89193-4558

Inside back cover: *From ▷ Hopi Point, South Rim, after a summer storm. Photo by Larry Ulrich.*

Back cover: *From Hopi ▷ Point, after a winter storm. Photo by Kaz Hagiwara.*

Created, Designed and Published in the U.S.A.
Printed by Dong-A Printing and Publishing, Seoul, Korea
Color Separations by Kedia/Kwangyangsa Co., Ltd.